Published 1979 by Warwick Press, 730 Fifth Avenue,
New York, New York 10019
First published in Great Britain by
Angus and Robertson, 1978
Copyright © 1978 by Grisewood & Dempsey Ltd.
Printed in Italy by New Interlitho, Milan
6 5 4 3 2 1   All rights reserved
Library of Congress Catalog Card No. 78–68536
ISBN 0–531–09152–X lib. bdg.
ISBN 0–531–09141–4

The Kangaroo

Story by
ANITA TOWNSEND

Pictures by
MICHAEL ATKINSON

WARWICK PRESS

The evening star glowed in the warm night sky. The moon rose slowly, and in the distance a dingo howled. The kangaroo raised her head from grazing, leaned back on her tail and listened.

The other kangaroos stirred and listened too. But the dingoes were not hungry. There was nothing to fear. Swooping bats chased insects, and the kangaroos continued to graze.

Two males were restless that night. The female kangaroo was ready to mate. Both of the big red males wanted to mate with her. So the two animals challenged each other to fight.

They stood upright facing each other, balancing on their strong tails, with their hind legs spread wide apart. They licked their own necks to release a red dye which spread over the pale fur of their chests. The rosy-pink glow made them look even more frightening. The fight was on.

The female watched as the males grasped each other with their forepaws, and kicked out with their great hind feet. They clawed and bit and boxed and scratched each other.

Then for a moment they drew back, tired and panting. They licked their forearms to cool themselves, then started again. At last one kangaroo struck his rival a savage kick. His sharp claw ripped into his rival's stomach. The beaten kangaroo limped away.

The winner hopped over to the female.
At first she ran off. But he chased her and
soon caught her. They stroked each other
with their forepaws and nuzzled each other.
Then they mated.

One month later, the female kangaroo was ready to give birth to her baby. She did not need to find a cave to shelter it. She had a pouch on her belly that would make a safe home for the young kangaroo.

First the kangaroo found a shady bush to rest under. She licked her belly and cleaned inside her pouch. Then she waited for the baby to be born. The tiny male kangaroo was less than an inch long and had no fur at all. Using his front paws the joey climbed up the fur on his mother's belly. Within three minutes he was safely in her pouch.

The baby kangaroo stayed in the warm darkness of his mother's pouch, growing fat and woolly, until he was about six months old. He sucked milk from one of the teats in the pouch.

After a while, the joey was big enough to poke his head out of the pouch and look at the world around him. His mother leaned forward on her front paws to graze. The joey smelt the juicy grass and nibbled at a tuft. The taste was good. He reached down for another. But, too late, he was jerked back into the pouch as his mother hopped away to rejoin the others.

Soon the bumpy ride was over. Peeking from the pouch, the joey looked at the others. Some were lying, sunbathing and playing lazy little games. Some were resting in the shade of a gum tree watching the lizards.

The joey saw a frilled lizard sitting on a big flat stone, warming itself in the sun. Then the air was filled with glittering wings and excited chatter. He looked up and saw a flock of brilliant green and yellow budgerigars. The mother kangaroo settled down to sleep. And after a while the joey slid back into the pouch and went to sleep too.

Next day the joey grew bolder, and hopped right out of his mother's pouch. He ate a mouthful of grass and hopped away to find some more.

But he did not go far. As he bent to bite the leaves, he caught sight of a large brown snake. It was coiled up by a stone and was watching him. The joey jumped back in terror and bounded towards his mother. He leapt for the safety of her pouch, diving in headfirst. Once in the pouch, he twisted himself round and put his head out to see what was happening. But he was already on the move.

The adult kangaroos had also seen the snake and were bounding away as fast as they could.

As summer passed, the land grew hotter and drier. The joey was now too big to travel in his mother's pouch. Instead, he bounded along beside her, stopping sometimes to push his head into the pouch for a drink of milk.

One day a strange smell came on the
wind. The kangaroos moved away from the
smell, but it grew stronger and stronger.
Small birds and flocks of cockatoos flew
ahead of them. The kangaroo hopped away,
faster and faster. It took all the joey's strength
to keep up with her. The smell grew stronger.
A fine hot ash fell from the sky, and they
heard the terrifying roar and crackle of fire.

Snakes, lizards, skinks, bandicoots and little rat kangaroos fled in terror before the flames. A family of dingoes sped by, for once too frightened to stop for food. A herd of wallabies bounded past the kangaroos as the fire raced up behind. Now they could feel the fierce heat.

The kangaroo raced away, covering the hot ground in huge leaps. Her joey leapt along behind her. They soared over rocks and ant heaps.

At last they reached a waterhole fringed
with reeds. The joey was almost too weak to
stand, and he could no longer see his mother.
The other kangaroos plunged ahead of him
into the shallow water. Then suddenly he
caught sight of his mother waiting for him. He
hopped towards her and together they sped
into the water and felt it splash coolly over
their fur. The fire roared past but it did not
harm them. They were safe.

The sun sank and the cool of the evening settled over the lake. The joey watched a family of emus drink greedily. A pair of black swans swam slowly away from the shore; an avocet strutted in the water, watched by an egret and a brightly colored kingfisher. The dingo family loped off towards the distant hills. Soon the rains would come and the burnt land would spring to life again. Then the joey would return with his mother to their homeland.

Kangaroo Facts

Keen ears listen for enemies (although kangaroos now have few enemies apart from man)

Sharp eyes and a keen sense of smell keep the kangaroo alert to danger

Look at the kangaroo's head and see how very much like the head and jaws of a deer it is. Can you think why ? The answer is that, though they live in different parts of the world, they lead the same kind of life. They graze and browse on plants in similar ways. Their legs, however, are different because they move in different ways.

A Real Bounder

The story is about the red kangaroo, which lives on grasslands all over Australia. It is the largest of the kangaroos, with a weight of over 200 pounds. When standing upright on its huge back feet and supporting itself with its massive tail, it may be as much as six feet tall. The back legs are much larger than the front ones and the animal uses them to move along with great bounds. It can cover over 20 feet with a single bound.

Little Joey

The kangaroo is a marsupial. This means that the mother carries her young in a pouch. Although the kangaroo is a large animal, the newborn baby is really tiny. It is only about an inch long and hardly looks like an animal at all. It is a naked, pink, bean-shaped object with a mouth at one end and a pair of tiny clawed feet. Guided by instinct, it crawls slowly into its mother's pouch and stays there for about six months, feeding on milk from its mother's body. The youngster is known as a joey.

Inside its mother's pouch, the tiny Joey clings fast to a teat and sucks the life-giving milk.

Roo's Relatives

The great gray kangaroo is about the same size as the red, but others are much smaller. Many of the smaller ones are called wallabies. The pademelons are even smaller, while the smallest of all are the rat kangaroos. The tree kangaroos spend their time eating leaves high in the trees.

Tree kangaroo

Rat kangaroo
(using its tail to carry nest material)

Pretty-face wallaby

Short-tailed pademelon

Two red kangaroos:
(the male is red and the female is grayish)

Great gray kangaroo, with her Joey